salsas, dips & relishes

salsas, dips & relishes

SILVANA FRANCO

LORENZ BOOKS

For all recipes, **quantities** are given in both **metric** & **imperial** measures &, where appropriate, measures are also given in **standard cups** & **spoons**. Follow one set, but not a mixture, because they are **not interchangeable**.

Standard **spoon** & **cup measures** are level.
1 tsp = 5ml, 1 tbsp = 15ml, 1 cup = 250ml/8fl oz

Australian standard **tablespoons** are 20ml. Australian readers should use 3 tsp in place of 1 tbsp for measuring small quantities of gelatine, cornflour, salt,etc.

Medium (US large) **eggs** are used unless otherwise stated.

Some of the recipes in this book previously appeared in *Salsas, Relishes and Dips.*

First published in 2001 by Lorenz Books
Lorenz Books is an imprint of Anness Publishing Limited
Hermes House, 88–89 Blackfriars Road, London SE1 8HA.
www.lorenzbooks.com

This edition distributed in Canada by Raincoast Books,
9050 Shaughnessy Street, Vancouver, British Columbia V6P 6EG

© Anness Publishing Limited 2001

Published in the USA by Lorenz Books
Anness Publishing Inc., 27 West 20th Street, New York, NY 10011

A CIP catalogue record for this book is available from the British Library.

Publisher Joanna Lorenz
Managing Editor Linda Fraser
Editor Rebecca Clunes
Copy editor Catherine Humby
Design Norma Martin
Photography William Lingwood, Simon Smith
Recipes by Silvana Franco, Jane Milton and Brian Glover
Production controller Joanna King

10 9 8 7 6 5 4 3 2 1

salsas, dips & relishes

introduction

Salsas, dips and **relishes** enliven eating and make food fun. Offer them with plain dishes, such as **fish** or **chops**, spoon them into **piping-hot** baked **potatoes**, use to top sandwich fillings, or simply serve them with a bowl of **tortilla chips**. The versatility of these tasty sauces makes them a valuable addition to every meal. All of these recipes are simple to make and are based on **fresh fruit** and vegetables combined with flavourings such as **herbs, garlic** and **fresh chillies**. Be adventurous – adapt the recipe to **suit** your store cupboard or pantry, or **personal taste**. However you choose to serve it, a little salsa is sure to add a sparkle to your meals.

serving suggestions

SALSAS, DIPS AND RELISHES ARE **WONDERFULLY VERSATILE**: SPOON OVER **MEAT**, **FISH** OR **CHICKEN** DISHES, USE AS A **SANDWICH FILLING**, OR SERVE WITH **ANTIPASTI** OR **CHEESE**. ONE OF THE **BEST** WAYS TO ENJOY THEM IS WITH A SELECTION OF TITBITS FOR DIPPING.

bread sticks

Choose Italian-style bread sticks for thick and creamy dips. To serve, pile the bread sticks on a plate or stand in a tall glass or jug (pitcher).

cheese straws

These are ideal for dipping and dunking. You can buy cheese straws ready-made, but they are also very easy to make at home. Simply roll out a small packet of puff pastry thinly and cut into strips. Brush the strips with beaten egg and sprinkle with a little grated cheese. (Twist the strips first, if you like.) Chill for 10 minutes, then bake at 180°C/350°F/Gas 4 for 15–20 minutes or until the straws are puffed and golden. Cool on a wire rack before serving.

Top row: **bread sticks and cheese straws**
Middle row: **fruit crudités and vegetable crudités**
Bottom row: **tortilla chips, potato crisps (US potato chips), corn chips, vegetable crisps (US vegetable chips)**

fruit crudités

These are the perfect accompaniment to sweet dips. Cut chunks of banana, apple, peach, pear or nectarine and arrange on a platter with strawberries, segments of oranges or satsumas, plums, sharon fruit or not-too-ripe figs.

vegetable crudités

Fresh raw vegetables make wonderful scoops for all manner of dips and salsas. Try sticks of cucumber, carrot and celery or trim small florets of cauliflower or broccoli. To make "scoops", cut small peppers lengthways, trim celery into short lengths, or cut pieces of cucumber into quarters and remove the seeds. Crisp central lettuce leaves or chicory (Belgian endive) leaves also make delicious crudités.

tortilla chips

The classic accompaniment to chilled tomato salsa, tortilla chips are now available in a wide variety of flavours. Serve the fiery hot tortilla chips with creamy dips and the cool ones with more robust salsas and relishes.

potato crisps

Salted crisps (US potato chips), either the plain variety or one of the many flavours are great served with any dip. Choose thicker crisps for chunky or very thick dips and only serve light, creamy dips with the more fragile varieties.

corn chips

These Mexican-style snacks are widely available. Choose cheese-flavoured chips for creamy dips and the plain variety for tomato salsas. Also good are the tasty blue corn chips.

vegetable crisps

Although available to buy, vegetable crisps (US vegetable chips) are easy to make at home. Sweet potato, beetroot (beet), carrot, parsnip and, of course, potato all work well. Peel the vegetables, slice them wafer-thin with a mandoline or swivel-style vegetable peeler, then deep-fry in hot vegetable oil. Season with salt and a little chilli powder, paprika or cayenne pepper.

instant dips

WHIP UP SOME **SPEEDY DIPS** FOR AN **IMPROMPTU PARTY** OR TO IMPRESS **UNEXPECTED GUESTS** WITH THE HELP OF **STORE CUPBOARD OR PANTRY CLASSICS**, SUCH AS MAYONNAISE, SUN-DRIED TOMATOES AND SOY SAUCE.

tangy crème fraîche dip

Stir a finely chopped bunch of spring onions (scallions) into a carton of crème fraîche. Add a dash of chilli sauce and a squeeze of fresh lime juice. Serve with tortilla chips.

sun-dried tomato dip

Stir one or two tablespoons of sun-dried tomato paste into a carton of Greek (US strained plain) yogurt. Season to taste with salt and ground black pepper. Serve with small triangles of toasted pitta bread or salted crisps (US potato chips).

spiced yogurt dip

To make a delicious and speedy Indian-style dip, stir a little mild or hot and spicy curry paste into a carton of natural (plain) yogurt. Add a finely chopped apple or a spoonful or two of mango chutney. Serve with crisp poppadums.

tomato and horseradish dip

Bring a little tang to a small carton or bottle of passata (strained tomatoes) by adding some horseradish sauce. Season to taste and serve with spicy tortilla chips.

pesto dip

Stir a tablespoon of ready-made red or green pesto into a carton of sour cream for a quick, Italian-style dip. Serve with crudités or wedges of roasted Mediterranean vegetables, such as red (bell) peppers and courgettes (zucchini).

yogurt and grainy mustard dip

Mix a small carton of Greek (US strained plain) yogurt with one or two teaspoons of wholegrain mustard. Serve with grissini or crudités.

black olive dip

To make a great dip for bread sticks, stir a little black olive paste into a carton of extra thick double (heavy) cream until smooth. Add a squeeze of fresh lemon juice and season to taste. Serve chilled.

Clockwise from top right: **tangy crème fraîche dip; sun-dried tomato dip; spiced yogurt dip; tomato and horseradish dip; pesto dip; yogurt and grainy mustard dip; black olive dip.** Middle: (top) **herby mayonnaise;** (bottom) **creamy chive dip**

herby mayonnaise

Liven up ready-made French-style mayonnaise with a handful of chopped fresh herbs – try flat leaf parsley, basil, dill, chives, mint, coriander or tarragon. Season to taste with salt and plenty of ground black pepper. Serve with chips (French fries) or crisp vegetable batons such as celery, carrot and cucumber. This dip is also good made with sour cream in place of the mayonnaise.

creamy chive dip

For a simple, speedy dip, mix a tub of soft cheese (farmer's cheese) with two or three tablespoons of chopped fresh chives and season to taste with salt and black pepper. If the dip is a little too thick, stir in a spoonful or two of milk to soften it. Serve with spicy tortilla chips, corn chips and bread sticks.

fast & fiery

ingredients

2 ripe **avocados**

2 **red chillies**, seeded

1 **garlic** clove

1 **shallot**

30ml/2 tbsp **olive oil**, plus extra
   to serve

juice of 1 **lemon**

salt

flat leaf **parsley** leaves,
   to garnish

guacamole

NACHOS OR PLAIN **TORTILLA CHIPS** ARE
THE PERFECT ACCOMPANIMENT FOR THIS
CLASSIC MEXICAN DIP.

variation

Make a completely smooth guacamole by whizzing the ingredients in a blender or
food processor. For a chunkier version, add a diced tomato or red (bell) pepper.

method

SERVES 4

1 Halve the avocados, remove their stones and, using a spoon, scoop out
their flesh into a bowl.

2 Mash the flesh well with a potato masher or a large fork.

3 Finely chop the chillies, garlic and shallot, then stir into the mashed
avocado with the olive oil and lemon juice. Add salt to taste.

4 Spoon the mixture into a small serving bowl. Drizzle over a little olive
oil and scatter with a few flat leaf parsley leaves. Serve immediately.

saucy tomato dip

method

THIS **VERSATILE** DIP IS DELICIOUS SERVED WITH **ABSOLUTELY ANYTHING** AND CAN BE MADE UP TO 24 HOURS **IN ADVANCE**.

1 Peel and halve the shallot and garlic cloves. Place in a blender or food processor with the basil leaves, then process the ingredients until they are very finely chopped.

2 Halve the tomatoes and add to the shallot mixture. Pulse the power until the mixture is well blended and the tomatoes are finely chopped.

3 With the motor still running, slowly pour in the olive oil. Add salt and pepper to taste.

4 Halve the chillies lengthways and remove their seeds. Finely slice them across into tiny strips and stir them into the tomato mixture. Serve at room temperature. Garnish with a few torn basil leaves.

ingredients

1 **shallot**

2 **garlic** cloves

handful of fresh **basil** leaves, plus extra to garnish

500g/1¼lb ripe **tomatoes**

30ml/2 tbsp **olive oil**

2 **green chillies**

salt and ground **black pepper**

---

cook's tip

This dip is best made with full-flavoured sun-ripened tomatoes. In winter, use a drained 400g/14oz can of plum tomatoes.

mango & radish salsa

THE SWEET FLAVOUR AND **JUICY TEXTURE** OF MANGO IN THIS SALSA **CONTRASTS** VERY WELL WITH THE HOT AND CRUNCHY RADISHES. SIMPLY SERVE WITH GRILLED **FISH** OR **CHICKEN**.

ingredients

1 large, ripe **mango**
12 **radishes**
juice of 1 **lemon**
45ml/3 tbsp **olive oil**
red **Tabasco sauce,** to taste
45ml/3 tbsp chopped fresh
   coriander (cilantro)
5ml/1 tsp **pink peppercorns**
salt

variation
Try using papaya in place of the mango in this salsa.

method

SERVES 4

1 Holding the mango upright on a chopping board, use a large knife to slice the flesh away from either side of the large flat stone in two pieces. Using a smaller knife, carefully trim away any flesh still clinging to the top and bottom of the stone.

2 Score the flesh of the mango halves deeply, taking care to avoid cutting through the skin: make parallel incisions about 1cm/½in apart; turn and cut lines in the opposite direction. Carefully turn the skin inside out so the flesh stands out like hedgehog spikes. Slice the diced flesh away from the skin.

3 Trim the radishes, discarding the root tails and leaves. Coarsely grate the radishes or dice them finely and place them in a bowl with the mango cubes.

4 Stir the lemon juice and olive oil with salt and a few drops of Tabasco sauce to taste, then stir in the chopped coriander.

5 Coarsely crush the pink peppercorns with a pestle and mortar or place them on a chopping board and flatten them with the heel of a heavy-bladed knife. Stir into the lemon oil.

6 Toss the radishes and mango, pour in the dressing and toss again. Chill for up to 2 hours before serving.

ingredients

2–4 **green chillies**

8 **spring onions** (scallions)

2 **garlic** cloves

50g/2oz **salted capers**

fresh **tarragon** sprig

bunch of fresh **parsley**

grated rind and juice of 1 **lime**

juice of 1 **lemon**

90ml/6 tbsp **olive oil**

about 15ml/1 tbsp **green Tabasco sauce**, to taste

ground **black pepper**

salsa verde

THERE ARE **MANY VERSIONS** OF THIS **CLASSIC** GREEN SALSA. SERVE THIS ONE WITH **CREAMY** MASHED POTATOES OR DRIZZLED OVER **CHARGRILLED** SQUID.

method

SERVES 4

1 Halve the chillies and remove their seeds. Trim the spring onions and halve the garlic, then place in a food processor. Pulse the power briefly until all the ingredients are roughly chopped.

2 Use your fingertips to rub the excess salt off the capers but do not rinse them (see Variation, below). Add the capers, tarragon and parsley to the food processor and pulse again until these ingredients are quite finely chopped.

3 Transfer the mixture to a small bowl. Stir in the lime rind and juice, lemon juice and olive oil. Stir the mixture lightly so the citrus juice and oil do not emulsify.

4 Add green Tabasco and black pepper to taste. Chill until ready to serve. This salsa tastes much better fresh, so do not prepare more than 8 hours in advance.

variation

If you can find only capers pickled in vinegar, they can be used for this salsa but must be rinsed well in cold water first.

avocado & red pepper salsa

THIS SIMPLE SALSA IS A **FIRE-AND-ICE** MIXTURE OF **HOT** CHILLI AND **COOLING** AVOCADO. SERVE WITH CORN CHIPS OR TORTILLA CHIPS FOR **DIPPING**.

method

1 Halve and stone the avocados. Scoop out and finely dice the flesh. Finely chop the red onion.

2 Slice the top off the pepper and pull out the central core. Shake out any remaining seeds. Cut the pepper into thin strips and then into fine dice.

3 Halve the chillies, remove their seeds and finely chop the flesh. Mix the chillies, coriander, oil, lemon and salt and pepper to taste.

4 Place the avocado, red onion and pepper in a bowl. Pour in the chilli and coriander dressing and toss the mixture well. Serve immediately.

ingredients

2 ripe **avocados**
1 **red onion**
1 **red** (bell) **pepper**
4 **green chillies**
30ml/2 tbsp chopped fresh
    coriander (cilantro)
30ml/2 tbsp **sunflower oil**
juice of 1 **lemon**
salt and ground **black pepper**

cook's tip

The cut surfaces of avocados discolour very quickly, so if you plan to prepare this salsa in advance, make sure the avocados are coated with fresh lemon juice to help prevent discoloration.

ingredients

6 **habanero** or **Scotch bonnet chillies**

2 ripe **tomatoes**

4 **green jalapeño chillies**

30ml/2 tbsp chopped fresh **parsley**

30ml/2 tbsp **olive oil**

15ml/1 tbsp **balsamic** or **sherry vinegar**

salt

variation
Habanero chillies are among the hottest fresh chillies available. You may prefer to tone down the heat of this salsa by using a milder variety.

double chilli salsa

THIS IS A **SCORCHINGLY** HOT SALSA FOR ONLY THE **VERY BRAVE**! SPREAD **SPARINGLY** ON TO COOKED MEATS AND **BURGERS**.

method

SERVES 4–6

1 Skewer an habanero or Scotch bonnet chilli on a metal fork and hold it in a gas flame for 2–3 minutes, turning until the skin blackens and blisters. Repeat with all the habanero or Scotch bonnet chillies.

2 Skewer the tomatoes one at a time and hold them in the flame for 1–2 minutes, until the skin splits and wrinkles.

3 Carefully slip off the tomato skins, then halve the tomatoes and use a teaspoon to scoop out and discard the seeds. Chop the flesh very finely and set aside.

4 Using a clean dish towel, gently rub the blistered skins off all the habanero or Scotch bonnet chillies.

5 Try not to touch the chillies with your bare hands: use a fork to hold them and slice them open with a sharp knife. Scrape out and discard the seeds, then finely chop the flesh.

6 Halve the jalapeño chillies, remove their seeds and finely slice them widthways into tiny strips. Mix together both types of chillies, the tomatoes and chopped parsley.

7 Mix the olive oil, vinegar and a little salt, pour this over the salsa and cover the dish. Chill for up to 3 days.

piquant pineapple relish

method

THIS DELICIOUS **SWEET-AND-SOUR** RELISH IS EXCELLENT SERVED WITH **CHICKEN** OR CRISPY **BACON**.

1 Drain the pineapple and reserve 60ml/4 tbsp of the juice. Place the juice in a small pan with the sugar and vinegar.

2 Heat the juice mixture gently, stirring, until the sugar dissolves. Remove from the heat and add salt and pepper to taste.

3 Finely chop the garlic and spring onions. Halve the chillies, remove their seeds and finely chop the flesh. Finely shred the basil leaves.

4 Place the pineapple, garlic, spring onions and chillies in a bowl. Mix well and pour in the sauce. Allow to cool for 5 minutes, then stir in the shredded basil.

variation

This relish tastes extra special when made with fresh pineapple. If you do make it this way, simply substitute the juice of a freshly squeezed orange for the canned pineapple juice.

ingredients

400g/14oz can crushed
  pineapple in natural juice
30ml/2 tbsp light **muscovado**
  (molasses) **sugar**
30ml/2 tbsp **wine vinegar**
1 **garlic** clove
4 **spring onions** (scallions)
2 **red chillies**
10 fresh **basil** leaves
salt and ground **black pepper**

fast & fiery • **19**

fiery citrus salsa

THIS VERY **UNUSUAL** FRUIT SALSA MAKES A **FANTASTIC** MARINADE FOR SHELLFISH AND IT IS ALSO **DELICIOUS** DRIZZLED OVER CHICKEN OR MEAT JUST COOKED ON A BARBECUE.

ingredients

1 **orange**
1 **green apple**
2 fresh **red chillies**
1 **garlic** clove
8 fresh **mint** leaves
juice of 1 **lemon**
salt and ground **black pepper**

variation
If you're feeling really fiery, don't seed the chillies. They will make the salsa particularly hot and fierce.

method

SERVES 4

1 Begin by slicing the bottom off the orange so that it will stand firmly on a chopping board.

2 Using a sharp knife, remove the orange peel by slicing from the top to the bottom of the fruit.

3 Hold the orange in one hand over a bowl. Slice towards the middle of the fruit, to one side of a segment, and then gently twist the knife to ease the segment away from the membrane and out of the orange. Repeat to remove all the segments.

4 Squeeze any juice from the remaining orange membrane into the bowl. Peel the apple, slice it into wedges and remove the core.

5 Halve the chillies and remove their seeds, then place them in a blender or food processor with the orange segments and juice, apple wedges, garlic and fresh mint.

6 Process the ingredients until they are finely chopped. Then, with the motor running, pour in the lemon juice.

7 Season to taste with a little salt and pepper. Pour into a bowl or small jug and serve immediately.

chunky cherry tomato salsa

SUCCULENT CHERRY TOMATOES AND **REFRESHING** CUCUMBER
FORM THE BASIS OF THIS CHUNKY **CHILLI** AND **DILL-SEASONED**
SALSA. SERVE WITH **ROAST** CHICKEN OR CHILLI CON CARNE.

ingredients

1 ridge **cucumber**
5ml/1 tsp **sea salt**
500g/1¼lb **cherry tomatoes**
1 **garlic** clove
1 **lemon**
45ml/3 tbsp **chilli oil**
2.5ml/½ tsp **dried chilli flakes**
30ml/2 tbsp chopped fresh **dill**
salt and ground **black pepper**

variation
Try flavouring this salsa with other
fragrant herbs, such as tarragon,
coriander (cilantro) or even mint.

method

SERVES 4

1 Trim the ends off the cucumber and cut it into 2.5cm/1in lengths,
then cut each piece lengthways into thin slices.

2 Arrange the cucumber slices in a colander and sprinkle them with the
sea salt. Leave for 5 minutes until the cucumber has wilted.

3 Wash the cucumber slices well under cold water, then drain and pat
them dry with kitchen paper.

4 Quarter the cherry tomatoes and place in a bowl with the wilted
cucumber. Finely chop the garlic.

5 Grate the lemon rind finely and place in a small jug with the juice from
the lemon, the chilli oil, chilli flakes, dill and garlic. Add salt and
pepper to taste, and whisk with a fork.

6 Pour the chilli oil dressing over the tomato and cucumber and toss
well. Leave to marinate at room temperature for at least 2 hours
before serving.

simple & spicy

ingredients

200ml/7fl oz/scant 1 cup
  coconut cream
60ml/4 tbsp **crunchy
  peanut butter**
5ml/1 tsp **Worcestershire
  sauce**
red Tabasco sauce, to taste
fresh **coconut** and sprigs of
  fresh **coriander** (cilantro), to
  garnish (optional)

---

cook's tip

Thick coconut milk can be
substituted for coconut cream;
coconut milk is usually packed in
400g/14oz cans, but take care
to buy an unsweetened variety
for this recipe.

satay sauce

THIS VERSION OF THE POPULAR PEANUT SAUCE
IS VERY **SPEEDY** AND IT TASTES **DELICIOUS**
WITH SKEWERS OF GRILLED CHICKEN. FOR
PARTIES, ARRANGE THE SKEWERS AROUND
A BOWL OF **WARM SAUCE**.

method   SERVES 4

1 Pour the coconut cream into a small pan and heat it gently over a low
heat for about 2 minutes.

2 Add the peanut butter and stir vigorously until it is blended into the
coconut cream. Continue to heat until the mixture has warmed through
but is not boiling.

3 Add the Worcestershire sauce and a dash of Tabasco to taste. Pour
into a serving bowl.

4 Use a swivel-bladed vegetable peeler to shave thin strips from a piece
of fresh coconut, if using, and use as a garnish with sprigs of fresh
coriander. Serve immediately.

feta cheese & black olive salsa

method

1 Separate the radicchio leaves and rinse them well in cold water. Roughly tear the leaves into small pieces.

2 Cut or break the feta into small cubes. Place the radicchio in a bowl with the feta and olive halves and toss well to mix together.

3 Finely chop the garlic and chilli, and sprinkle over the salsa with the chopped parsley, olive oil, balsamic vinegar and sea salt to taste. Mix together well and serve immediately.

THE **SALTY** FLAVOUR OF THE FETA CHEESE AND OLIVES IN THIS **CHUNKY** SALSA IS DELIGHTFULLY BALANCED BY THE **BITTER-TASTING** RADICCHIO.

ingredients

1 head of **radicchio**
250g/9oz **feta cheese**
150g/5oz **black olives**, halved
    and stoned
1 **garlic** clove
1 **red chilli**, seeded
45ml/3 tbsp chopped
    fresh **parsley**
30ml/2 tbsp **olive oil**
15ml/1 tbsp **balsamic vinegar**
sea salt

cook's tip
Choose unpitted olives such as Kalamata for this salsa – they tend to have a stronger flavour and more interesting texture than the mild, pitted varieties.

ingredients

2 **garlic** cloves

1 **onion**

2 **green chillies**

30ml/2 tbsp **vegetable oil**

5–10ml/1–2 tsp **hot chilli powder**

400g/14oz can **kidney beans**

75g/3oz mature **Cheddar cheese,** grated

1 **red chilli**, seeded

salt and ground **black pepper**

cook's tip

For a dip with a coarser texture, do not purée the beans, but mash with a potato masher instead.

chilli bean dip

THIS **CREAMY** BEAN DIP IS BEST SERVED WARM WITH **TRIANGLES** OF TOASTED PITTA BREAD OR A BOWL OF **CRUNCHY**, PLAIN TORTILLA CHIPS.

method

SERVES 4

1 Finely chop the garlic and onion. Seed and finely chop both of the green chillies.

2 Heat the oil in a large sauté pan or deep frying pan and add the garlic, onion, green chillies and chilli powder.

3 Cook gently for 5 minutes, stirring regularly, until the onions are softened and transparent, but not browned.

4 Drain the kidney beans, reserving the liquor. Blend all but 30ml/2 tbsp of the beans to a purée in a food processor.

5 Add the puréed beans to the pan with 30–45ml/2–3 tbsp of the reserved liquor. Heat gently, stirring to mix well.

6 Stir in the whole beans and the Cheddar cheese. Cook gently for about 2–3 minutes, stirring until the cheese melts. Add salt and pepper to taste.

7 Cut the red chilli into tiny strips. Spoon the dip into four individual serving bowls and scatter the chilli strips over the top. Serve warm.

spiced carrot dip

THIS IS A DELICIOUS **LOW-FAT** DIP WITH A **SWEET AND SPICY** FLAVOUR. SERVE WITH WHEAT CRACKERS OR **FIERY** TORTILLA CHIPS.

method

SERVES 4

1 Finely chop the onion. Peel and grate the carrots. Place the onion, carrots, orange rind and juice and curry paste in a small pan. Bring to the boil, cover and simmer for 10 minutes, until tender.

2 Process the mixture in a blender or food processor until smooth. Leave to cool completely.

3 Stir in the yogurt, then tear the basil leaves into small pieces and stir them into the carrot mixture.

4 Add the lemon juice, Tabasco, salt and pepper to taste. Serve within a few hours at room temperature. Garnish with grated carrot.

variation
Greek (US strained plain) yogurt or sour cream may be used in place of the natural yogurt to make a richer, creamy dip.

ingredients

1 **onion**

3 **carrots**, plus extra to garnish

grated rind and juice of

2 **oranges**

15ml/1 tbsp **hot curry paste**

150ml/¼ pint/⅔ cup low-fat **natural** (plain) **yogurt**

handful of fresh **basil** leaves

15–30ml/1–2 tbsp fresh **lemon juice,** to taste

red Tabasco sauce, to taste

salt and ground **black pepper**

ingredients

400g/14oz can **chickpeas,**
   drained
2 **garlic** cloves
30ml/2 tbsp **tahini** or **smooth**
   peanut butter
60ml/4 tbsp **olive oil**
juice of 1 **lemon**
2.5ml/½ tsp **cayenne pepper**
15ml/1 tbsp **sesame seeds**
sea salt
lemon quarters and **herbs,**
   to garnish
hot buttered **toast**, to serve

cook's tip
Tahini is a thick, smooth and oily
paste made from sesame seeds. It is
available from health food shops and
large supermarkets. Tahini is a classic
ingredient in hummus, this Middle-
Eastern dip; peanut butter would not
be used in a traditional recipe but it
is a useful substitute.

hummus

THIS **NUTRITIOUS** DIP CAN BE SERVED WITH
VEGETABLE **CRUDITÉS** OR PACKED INTO
SALAD-FILLED PITTA, BUT IT IS **BEST
SPREAD THICKLY** ON HOT BUTTERED TOAST.

method

SERVES 4

1 Rinse the chickpeas well and place in a blender or food processor
with the garlic and a good pinch of sea salt.

2 Process the mixture until the chickpeas and garlic are very
finely chopped.

3 Add the tahini or peanut butter and process until fairly smooth. With
the motor still running, slowly pour in the oil and lemon juice.

4 Stir in the cayenne pepper and add more salt, if necessary. If the
mixture is too thick, stir in a little cold water. Transfer the hummus to
a serving bowl.

5 Heat a small non-stick frying pan and add the sesame seeds. Cook for
2–3 minutes, shaking the pan frequently, until the seeds are golden.
Remove the pan from the heat and allow to cool, then sprinkle over
the purée. Serve with toast and a garnish of lemon and herbs.

thai red curry sauce

method

SERVE THIS SAUCE WITH **SPRING ROLLS** AND **SPICY** INDONESIAN CRACKERS, OR TOSS IT INTO RICE **NOODLES** TO MAKE A TASTY ACCOMPANIMENT TO A **MAIN** MEAL.

1 Pour the coconut cream into a small bowl and stir in the Thai red curry paste.

2 Trim and finely slice the spring onions diagonally. Stir into the coconut cream with the coriander and chilli.

3 Stir in the soy sauce, lime juice, sugar, salt and pepper to taste. Pour the sauce into a small serving bowl.

4 Finely chop the dry-roasted peanuts and sprinkle them over the sauce. Serve immediately. Garnish with spring onions sliced lengthways.

variation
If you prefer, roasted cashew nuts can be substituted for the dry-roasted peanuts used here.

ingredients

200ml/7fl oz/scant 1 cup
  coconut cream
10–15ml/2–3 tsp **Thai red curry paste**
4 **spring onions** (scallions), plus extra, to garnish
30ml/2 tbsp chopped fresh **coriander** (cilantro)
1 **red chilli**, seeded and thinly sliced into rings
5ml/1 tsp **soy sauce**
juice of 1 **lime**
sugar, to taste
25g/1oz/¼ cup **dry-roasted peanuts**
salt and ground **black pepper**

cook's tip
The dip may be prepared in advance up to the end of step 3. Sprinkle the peanuts over just before serving.

ingredients

5cm/2in piece **fresh root ginger**

1 **onion**

2 **garlic** cloves

2 small **red chillies**, seeded

30ml/2 tbsp **sunflower oil**

5ml/1 tsp **cumin seeds**

150g/5oz/⅔ cup **red lentils**

250ml/8fl oz/1 cup **water**

15ml/1 tbsp **hot curry paste**

200ml/7fl oz/scant 1 cup **coconut cream**

juice of 1 **lemon**

handful of fresh **coriander** (cilantro) **leaves**

25g/1oz/¼ cup **flaked almonds**

salt and ground **black pepper**

variation

Try making this dhal with yellow split peas: they take longer to cook and a little extra water has to be added but the result is equally tasty.

lemon & coconut dhal

THIS CAN BE SERVED EITHER AS A **DIP** WITH **PITTA BREAD** OR AS A SPICY **SIDE DISH**.

method

SERVES 8

1 Use a vegetable peeler to peel the ginger and finely chop it with the onion, garlic and chillies.

2 Heat the oil in a large shallow pan. Add the ginger, onion, garlic, chillies and cumin seeds. Cook for 5 minutes, stirring occasionally until they are softened but not coloured.

3 Stir the lentils, water and curry paste into the pan. Bring to the boil, cover and cook gently over a low heat for 15–20 minutes, stirring occasionally, until the lentils are just tender and not yet broken.

4 Stir in all but 30ml/2 tbsp of the coconut cream. Bring to the boil and cook, uncovered, for a further 15–20 minutes, until the mixture is thick and pulpy. Remove from the heat, then stir in the lemon juice and the whole coriander leaves. Add salt and pepper to taste.

5 Heat a large frying pan and cook the flaked almonds for 1–2 minutes on each side until golden brown. Stir about three-quarters of the toasted almonds into the dhal.

6 Transfer the dhal to a serving bowl and swirl in the remaining coconut cream. Scatter the reserved almonds on top and serve warm.

sweet pepper salsa

ROASTING PEPPERS ENHANCES THEIR RICH
FLAVOUR AND GIVES THEM A **SOFT** TEXTURE.
SERVE WITH **POACHED SALMON**.

method

SERVES 4

1 Preheat the grill (broiler) to medium. Place the peppers on a baking
sheet and grill (broil) them for 8–10 minutes, turning regularly, until
their skins have blackened and are blistered.

2 Place the peppers in a bowl and cover with a clean dish towel. Leave
for 5 minutes so the steam helps to lift the skin away from the flesh.

3 Meanwhile, place the cumin seeds in a small frying pan. Heat gently,
stirring constantly, until the cumin seeds start to splutter and release
their aroma.

4 Remove the pan from the heat, then tip out the seeds into a mortar
and crush them lightly with a pestle.

5 When the peppers are cool enough to handle, pierce a hole in the
bottom of each and squeeze out all of the juices into a bowl.

6 Peel and core the peppers, discarding the seeds, then process the
flesh in a blender or food processor with the chilli and coriander until
finely chopped.

7 Stir in the olive oil, red wine vinegar and cumin seeds. Season with
salt and ground black pepper to taste. This salsa should be served at
room temperature.

ingredients

1 **red** (bell) **pepper**
1 **yellow** (bell) **pepper**
5ml/1 tsp **cumin seeds**
1 **red chilli**, seeded
30ml/2 tbsp chopped fresh
   coriander (cilantro)
30ml/2 tbsp **olive oil**
15ml/1 tbsp **red wine vinegar**
salt and ground **black pepper**

cook's tip

Choose red, yellow or orange
peppers for this salsa as the green
variety is less sweet.

cannellini bean dip

THIS **SOFT BEAN DIP** OR PÂTÉ IS VERY GOOD SPREAD ON WHEATEN CRACKERS OR **TOASTED ENGLISH MUFFINS**. ALTERNATIVELY, IT CAN BE SERVED WITH WEDGES OF TOMATO AND A **GREEN SALAD**.

ingredients

400g/14oz can **cannellini beans**
grated rind and juice of
  1 **lemon**
30ml/2 tbsp **olive oil**
1 **garlic** clove, finely chopped
30ml/2 tbsp chopped
  fresh **parsley**
red Tabasco sauce, to taste
cayenne pepper
salt and ground **black pepper**

method

SERVES 4

1 Drain the beans in a sieve and rinse them well under cold water. Transfer to a shallow bowl.

2 Use a potato masher to roughly purée the beans, then stir in the lemon and olive oil.

3 Stir in the chopped garlic and parsley. Add Tabasco sauce and salt and pepper to taste.

4 Spoon the mixture into a small bowl and dust lightly with cayenne pepper. Chill until ready to serve.

---

variation

Other beans can be used for this dip, for example butter (lima) beans or kidney beans.

ingredients

2 fresh **red chillies**

2 ripe **mangoes**

½ **white onion**

small bunch of **fresh coriander**
  (cilantro)

grated rind and juice of 1 **lime**

mango salsa

THIS HAS A FRESH, **FRUITY TASTE** AND IS
PERFECT WITH FISH OR AS A **CONTRAST** TO
RICH, CREAMY DISHES. THE **BRIGHT
COLOURS** MAKE IT AN ATTRACTIVE
ACCOMPANIMENT TO ANY MEAL.

method
SERVES 4

1 To peel the chillies spear them on a long-handled metal skewer and
roast them over the flame of a gas burner until the skins blister and
darken. Do not let the flesh burn. Alternatively, dry-fry them in a
griddle pan until the skins are scorched.

2 Place the roasted chillies in a strong plastic bag and tie the top to
keep the steam in. Set aside for 20 minutes.

3 Meanwhile, put one of the mangoes on a board and cut off a thick
slice close to the flat side of the stone. Turn the mango round and
repeat on the other side. Score the flesh on each thick slice with
criss-cross lines at 1cm/½in intervals, taking care not to cut through
the skin. Repeat with the second mango.

4 Fold the mango halves inside out so that the mango flesh stands
proud of the skin, in neat dice. Carefully slice these off the skin and
into a bowl. Cut off the flesh adhering to each stone, dice it and add it
to the bowl.

5 Remove the roasted chillies from the bag and carefully peel off the
skins. Cut off the stalks, then slit the chillies and scrape out the seeds.

6 Chop the white onion and the coriander finely and add them to the
diced mango. Chop the chilli flesh finely and add it to the mixture in
the bowl, together with the lime rind and juice. Stir well to mix, cover
and chill for at least 1 hour before serving. The salsa will keep for
2–3 days in the refrigerator.

black bean salsa

THIS SALSA HAS A PARTICULARLY **STRIKING APPEARANCE**. IT IS RARE TO FIND A BLACK SAUCE AND IT PROVIDES A **WONDERFUL CONTRAST** TO THE MORE COMMON REDS AND GREENS ON THE **PLATE**. LEAVE THE SALSA FOR A DAY OR TWO AFTER MAKING TO ALLOW THE **FLAVOURS** TO DEVELOP FULLY.

method

SERVES 4

1 Drain the black beans and put them in a large pan. Pour in water to cover and place the lid on the pan. Bring to the boil, lower the heat slightly and simmer the beans for about 40 minutes or until tender. They should still have a little bite and should not have begun to disintegrate. Drain, rinse under cold water, then drain again and leave the beans until cold.

2 Soak the dried chilli in hot water for about 10 minutes until softened. Drain, remove the stalk, then slit the chilli, scrape out the seeds with a small sharp knife and discard. Chop the flesh finely.

3 Spear the red chillies on a long-handled metal skewer and roast them over the flame of a gas burner until the skins blister and darken. Do not let the flesh burn. Alternatively, dry-fry them in a griddle pan until the skins are scorched. Then place the roasted chillies in a strong plastic bag and tie the top to keep the steam in. Set aside for 20 minutes.

4 Meanwhile, chop the red onion finely. Remove the chillies from the bag and peel off the skins. Slit them, remove the seeds and chop them finely.

5 Tip the beans into a bowl and add the onion and both types of chilli. Stir in the lime rind and juice, beer, oil and coriander. Season with salt and mix well. Chill before serving.

ingredients

130g/4½oz/generous ½ cup
  black beans, soaked
  overnight in water
  to cover
1 **dried chilli**
2 **red chillies**
1 **red onion**
grated rind and juice of 1 **lime**
30ml/2 tbsp **Mexican beer**
  (optional)
15ml/1 tbsp **olive oil**
small bunch of fresh **coriander**,
  (cilantro) chopped
salt

> ### cook's tip
> Dried chillies are a convenient store cupboard stand-by, and simply need soaking in water before use. The flavour of the chilli intensifies with the drying process.

ingredients

130g/4½oz **raw pumpkin seeds**

500g/1¼lb **tomatoes**

2 **garlic** cloves, crushed

300ml/½ pint/1¼ cups **chicken stock**, preferably freshly made

15ml/1 tbsp **vegetable oil**

45ml/3 tbsp **red chilli sauce**

salt (optional)

cook's tip

When dry-frying the pumpkin seeds, don't stop stirring for a moment or they may scorch, which would make the sauce bitter. It is a good idea to stand back a little as some of the hot seeds may fly out of the pan.

pumpkin seed relish

THIS **TRADITIONAL MEXICAN** RECIPE IS BASED UPON PUMPKIN SEEDS, AND HAS A DELICIOUS **NUTTY FLAVOUR**. IT IS **DELICIOUS** SERVED WITH COOKED CHICKEN OR RACK OF LAMB.

method

SERVES 4

1 Preheat the oven to 200°C/400°F/Gas 6. Heat a heavy-based frying pan until very hot.

2 Add the pumpkin seeds and dry-fry them, stirring constantly over the heat. The seeds will start to swell and pop, but they must not be allowed to scorch (see Cook's Tip).

3 When all the seeds have popped remove the pan from the heat.

4 Cut the tomatoes into quarters and place them on a baking tray. Roast in the hot oven for 45 minutes–1 hour, until charred and softened. Allow to cool slightly, then remove the skins using a small sharp knife.

5 Put the pumpkin seeds in a food processor and process until smooth. Add the tomatoes and process for a few minutes, then add the garlic and stock and process for 1 minute more.

6 Heat the oil in a large frying pan. Add the red chilli sauce and cook, stirring constantly, for 2–3 minutes. Add the pumpkin seed mixture and bring to the boil, stirring constantly.

7 Simmer the sauce for 20 minutes, stirring frequently until the sauce has thickened and reduced by about half.

8 Taste the salsa and add salt, if needed. Serve over meat or vegetables or cool and chill. The salsa will keep for up to 1 week in a covered bowl in the refrigerator.

bloody mary relish

SERVE THIS PERFECT **PARTY** SALSA WITH STICKS OF CRUNCHY CUCUMBER OR, ON A REALLY **SPECIAL OCCASION**, WITH FRESHLY SHUCKED **OYSTERS**.

---

variation
Whizz one or two fresh seeded, red chillies with the tomatoes instead of adding Tabasco sauce.

---

ingredients

4 ripe **tomatoes**

1 **celery** stalk

1 **garlic** clove

2 **spring onions** (scallions)

45ml/3 tbsp **tomato juice**

Worcestershire sauce, to taste

red Tabasco sauce, to taste

10ml/2 tsp **horseradish sauce**

15ml/1 tbsp **vodka**

juice of 1 **lemon**

salt and ground **black pepper**

method

1 Halve the tomatoes, celery and garlic. Trim the spring onions.

2 Process the vegetables in a blender or food processor until very finely chopped, then transfer them to a bowl.

3 Stir in the tomato juice and add a few drops of Worcestershire sauce and Tabasco to taste.

4 Stir in the horseradish sauce, vodka and lemon juice. Add salt and ground black pepper, to taste.

cool & creamy

butternut squash & parmesan dip

THE RICH, **NUTTY FLAVOUR** OF BUTTERNUT SQUASH IS BROUGHT OUT TO THE FULL WHEN IT IS **ROASTED**. SERVE THIS DIP WITH **MELBA TOAST** OR **CHEESE STRAWS**.

ingredients

1 **butternut squash**
15g/½oz/1 tbsp **butter**
4 **garlic** cloves, unpeeled
30ml/2 tbsp freshly grated
   Parmesan cheese
45–75ml/3–5 tbsp **double**
   (heavy) **cream**
salt and ground **black pepper**

cook's tip
If you don't have a blender or food processor, simply mash the squash in a bowl using a potato masher, then beat in the grated cheese and cream using a wooden spoon.

method

SERVES 4

1 Preheat the oven to 200°C/400°F/Gas 6. Halve the butternut squash lengthways, then scoop out and discard the seeds.

2 Use a small, sharp knife to deeply score the flesh in a criss-cross pattern: cut as close to the skin as possible, but take care not to cut through it.

3 Arrange both halves in a small roasting tin and dot them with the butter. Sprinkle with salt and pepper and roast for 20 minutes.

4 Tuck the unpeeled garlic cloves around the squash in the roasting tin and continue baking for 20 minutes, until the pumpkin squash is tender and softened.

5 Scoop the flesh out of the squash shells and place it in a blender or food processor. Slip the garlic cloves out of their skins and add to the squash. Process until smooth.

6 With the motor running, add all but 5ml/1 tsp of the Parmesan cheese and then the cream. Check the seasoning and spoon the dip into a serving bowl: it is at its best served warm. Scatter the reserved cheese over the dip.

variation
Try making this dip with pumpkin or other types of squash, such as acorn squash or New Zealand kabocha.

ingredients

150g/5oz **blue cheese**, such as
Stilton or **Danish Blue**

150g/5oz/⅔ cup **soft white**
(farmer's) **cheese**

75ml/5 tbsp **Greek** (US strained
plain) **yogurt**

salt and ground **black pepper**

cook's tip
This is a very thick dip to which you
can add a little more yogurt, or stir in
a little milk, for a softer consistency.

blue cheese dip

THIS DIP CAN BE MIXED UP IN **NEXT TO
NO TIME** AND IS DELICIOUS SERVED WITH
CRISP-TEXTURED FRESH PEARS. ADD MORE
YOGURT TO MAKE A GREAT **DRESSING** FOR
A CELERY, APPLE AND WALNUT SALAD.

method

SERVES 4

1 Crumble the blue cheese into a bowl. Using a wooden spoon, beat the
cheese to soften it.

2 Add the soft cheese to the bowl and beat the mixture well to blend
the two cheeses together.

3 Gradually beat in the yogurt, adding enough to give you the
consistency you prefer.

4 Season to taste with a little salt and lots of ground black pepper.
Place the dip in the refrigerator to chill until you are ready to serve.

thousand island dip

THIS VARIATION ON THE **CLASSIC** THOUSAND ISLAND DRESSING IS FAR REMOVED FROM THE **ORIGINAL VERSION**, BUT CAN BE SERVED IN THE SAME WAY – WITH COOKED SHELLFISH LACED ON TO **BAMBOO SKEWERS** FOR DIPPING OR WITH A SIMPLE MIXED FISH AND SHELLFISH SALAD.

method

SERVES 4

1 Drain the sun-dried tomatoes on kitchen paper to remove excess oil, then finely chop them.

2 Skewer each tomato in turn on a metal fork and hold in a gas flame for 1–2 minutes, until the skin wrinkles and splits. Slip off and discard the skins, then halve the tomatoes and scoop out the seeds with a teaspoon. Finely chop the tomato flesh.

3 Beat the soft cheese, then gradually beat in the mayonnaise and tomato purée.

4 Stir in most of the chopped parsley and all the sun-dried tomatoes, then add the chopped tomatoes and their seeds and mix well.

5 Add the lemon rind and juice and Tabasco sauce to taste. Stir in the Worcestershire or soy sauce, and season with salt and ground black pepper, to taste.

6 Transfer the dip to a serving bowl, cover and chill until you are ready to serve. Garnish with lemon rind and the remaining parsley.

ingredients

4 **sun-dried tomatoés** in oil

4 **tomatoes**

150g/5oz/⅔ cup **soft** (farmer's) **cheese**

60ml/4 tbsp **mayonnaise**

30ml/2 tbsp **tomato purée**

30ml/2 tbsp chopped fresh **parsley**

grated rind and juice of 1 **lemon**, plus extra grated rind to garnish

red Tabasco sauce, to taste

5ml/1 tsp **Worcestershire** or **soy sauce**

salt and ground **black pepper**

---

variation
Stir in cayenne pepper or a chopped fresh chilli for a more fiery dip.

tzatziki

SERVE THIS **CLASSIC** AND **REFRESHING** GREEK DIP WITH STRIPS OF TOASTED **PITTA BREAD**.

ingredients

1 **mini cucumber**
4 **spring onions** (scallions)
1 **garlic clove**
200ml/7fl oz/scant 1 cup **Greek**
   (US strained plain) **yogurt**
45ml/3 tbsp chopped fresh **mint**
fresh **mint** sprig, to garnish
   (optional)
salt and ground **black pepper**

---

cook's tip
Make sure you use Greek yogurt for this dip – it has a higher fat content than most yogurts, which gives it a deliciously rich, creamy texture.

---

method

SERVES 4

1 Trim the ends from the mini cucumber, then cut the main section into 5mm/¼in dice.

2 Trim the spring onions and garlic clove, then chop both very finely with a sharp knife.

3 Beat the yogurt until smooth, if necessary, then gently stir in the cucumber, onions, garlic and chopped mint.

4 Transfer the mixture to a serving bowl and add salt and plenty of ground black pepper to taste. Chill until ready to serve and then garnish with a small mint sprig, if you like.

ingredients

2 whole **garlic** heads

15ml/1 tbsp **olive oil**

60ml/4 tbsp **mayonnaise**

75ml/5 tbsp **Greek** (US strained plain) **yogurt**

5ml/1 tsp **wholegrain mustard**

salt and ground **black pepper**

cook's tip

If you are already cooking on a barbecue, leave the garlic heads whole and cook them on the hot barbecue until tender, then peel them and mash the flesh.

mellow garlic dip

TWO **WHOLE HEADS** OF GARLIC MAY SEEM LIKE A LOT BUT, ONCE **COOKED**, IT BECOMES SWEET AND **MELLOW**. SERVE WITH CRUNCHY BREAD STICKS, CRISPS OR CHIPS.

method

SERVES 4

1 Preheat the oven to 200°C/400°F/Gas 6. Separate the garlic cloves and place them in a small roasting pan.

2 Pour the olive oil over the garlic cloves and turn them with a spoon to coat them evenly with oil.

3 Roast for 20–30 minutes, until the garlic is tender and softened. Leave to cool for 5 minutes.

4 Trim off the root end of each roasted garlic clove. Peel the cloves and discard the skins.

5 Place the roasted garlic on a chopping board and sprinkle with salt. Mash with a fork until roughly puréed, then place in a small bowl and stir in the mayonnaise, yogurt and wholegrain mustard.

6 Taste and adjust the seasoning if necessary, then spoon the dip into a serving bowl. Cover and chill until ready to serve.

variation

For a low-fat version of this dip, use reduced-fat mayonnaise and low-fat natural (plain) yogurt.

creamy mediterranean dip

SPREAD THIS VELVET-TEXTURED DIP **THICKLY** ON TO TOASTED ROUNDS OF BREAD, THEN **TOP** WITH SLIVERS OF SUN-DRIED TOMATO TO MAKE **ITALIAN-STYLE** CROSTINI.

method

SERVES 4

1 Preheat the grill (broiler) to medium. Place the aubergine on a baking sheet and grill (broil) it for 20–30 minutes, turning occasionally, until the skin is blackened and the flesh feels soft when squeezed.

2 Cover the aubergine with a clean dish towel and leave it to cool for about 5 minutes.

3 Finely chop the onion and garlic. Heat the oil in a frying pan and cook the onion and garlic over a medium heat for 5 minutes, until softened, but not browned.

4 Peel and discard the skin of the aubergine, then chop roughly and place in a large bowl. Using a potato masher or a large fork mash the flesh of the aubergine to make a pulpy purée.

5 Stir in the onion and garlic, parsley and crème fraîche to the aubergine purée. Add the Tabasco sauce, lemon juice and salt and pepper to taste.

6 Transfer the dip to a serving bowl and serve warm or leave to cool and serve at room temperature.

ingredients

1 large **aubergine** (eggplant)
1 small **onion**
2 garlic **cloves**
30ml/2 tbsp **olive oil**
60ml/4 tbsp chopped
 fresh **parsley**
75ml/5 tbsp **crème fraîche**
red Tabasco sauce, to taste
juice of 1 **lemon**, to taste
salt and ground **black pepper**

> ### cook's tip
> The aubergine can be roasted in the oven at 200°C/400°F/Gas 6 for 20 minutes, if preferred.

sour cream cooler

THIS COOLING DIP IS A PERFECT **ACCOMPANIMENT** TO HOT AND **SPICY** MEXICAN DISHES. ALTERNATIVELY, SERVE IT AS A SNACK WITH THE FIERIEST **TORTILLA CHIPS** YOU CAN FIND.

ingredients

method

SERVES 2

1 small **yellow** (bell) **pepper**
2 small **tomatoes**
150ml/¼ pint/⅔ cup **sour cream**
grated **lemon** rind and chopped
  fresh **parsley**, to garnish

1 Halve the pepper lengthways. Remove the core and seeds, then cut the flesh into tiny dice.

2 Halve the tomatoes, then scoop out and discard the seeds and cut the flesh into tiny dice.

3 Stir the finely diced pepper and tomatoes into the sour cream and mix well.

4 Spoon the dip into a small bowl and chill. Garnish with grated lemon rind and chopped parsley before serving.

variation
For a change, use finely diced avocado or cucumber in place of the yellow pepper or tomatoes.

red onion raita

RAITA IS A **TRADITIONAL INDIAN** ACCOMPANIMENT FOR HOT CURRIES. IT IS ALSO DELICIOUS SERVED WITH **POPPADUMS** AS A DIP.

ingredients

5ml/1 tsp **cumin seeds**

1 small **garlic** clove

1 small **green chilli**, seeded

1 large **red onion**

150ml/¼ pint/⅔ cup **natural** (plain) **yogurt**

30ml/2 tbsp chopped fresh **coriander** (cilantro), plus extra to garnish

2.5ml/½ tsp **sugar**

salt

cook's tip
For an extra tangy raita stir in 15ml/1 tbsp lemon juice. To make a pretty garnish, reserve a few thin wedges of onion, before chopping the rest.

method

SERVES 4

1 Heat a small pan and dry-fry the cumin seeds for 1–2 minutes, until they release their aroma and begin to pop.

2 Lightly crush the seeds with a pestle and mortar or flatten them with the heel of a heavy-bladed knife.

3 Finely chop the garlic, chilli and red onion, reserving a few onion slices for the garnish. Stir into the yogurt with the crushed cumin seeds and chopped coriander.

4 Add sugar and salt to taste. Spoon the raita into a small bowl and chill until ready to serve. Garnish with extra coriander and the reserved onion slices before serving.

rich & robust

chilli relish

THIS **SPICY** RELISH WILL KEEP FOR AT LEAST A **WEEK** IN THE REFRIGERATOR. SERVE IT WITH **SAUSAGES** AND **BURGERS**.

ingredients

method

SERVES 8

6 **tomatoes**
1 **onion**
1 **red** (bell) **pepper**, seeded
2 **garlic** cloves
30ml/2 tbsp **olive oil**
5ml/1 tsp **ground cinnamon**
5ml/1 tsp **chilli flakes**
5ml/1 tsp ground **ginger**
5ml/1 tsp **salt**
2.5ml/½ tsp ground
   black pepper
75g/3oz/⅓ cup light **muscovado**
   (molasses) **sugar**
75ml/5 tbsp **cider vinegar**
handful of fresh **basil** leaves

1 Skewer each of the tomatoes in turn on a metal fork and hold in a gas flame for 1–2 minutes, turning until the skin splits and wrinkles. Slip off the skins, then roughly chop the tomatoes.

2 Roughly chop the onion, red pepper and garlic. Heat the oil in a pan. Add the onion, pepper and garlic to the pan.

3 Cook gently for 5–8 minutes, until the pepper is softened. Add the chopped tomatoes, cover and cook for 5 minutes, until the tomatoes release their juices.

4 Stir in the cinnamon, chilli flakes, ginger, salt, pepper, sugar and vinegar. Bring gently to the boil, stirring until the sugar dissolves.

5 Simmer, uncovered, for 20 minutes, until the mixture is pulpy. Stir in the basil leaves and check the seasoning.

6 Allow to cool completely then transfer to a glass jar or a plastic container with a tightly fitting lid. Store, covered, in the refrigerator.

---

cook's tip
This relish thickens slightly on cooling so do not worry if the mixture seems a little wet at the end of step 5.

ingredients

4 **spring onions** (scallions)

4cm/1½in piece **fresh**
   root ginger

2 **red chillies**

2 **garlic cloves**

60ml/4 tbsp **hoisin sauce**

120ml/4fl oz/½ cup **passata**
   (bottled strained tomatoes)

5ml/1 tsp **sesame oil** (optional)

cook's tip
Hoisin sauce makes an excellent
base for full-flavour dips, especially
when combining crunchy vegetables
and other Oriental seasonings.

oriental hoisin dip

THIS **SPEEDY** ORIENTAL DIP NEEDS NO
COOKING AND CAN BE MADE IN **JUST A FEW
MINUTES** — IT TASTES **GREAT** WITH TINY
SPRING ROLLS OR PRAWN CRACKERS. THIS
SAUCE IS ALSO **GOOD** WITH SKEWERS OF
GRILLED MEAT.

method
SERVES 4

1 Trim off and discard the green ends of the spring onions. Slice the
   remainder very thinly.

2 Peel the fresh root ginger with a swivel-bladed vegetable peeler,
   then chop it finely.

3 Halve the chillies lengthways and remove their seeds. Finely slice the
   flesh widthways into tiny strips. Finely chop the garlic.

4 Stir together the hoisin sauce, passata, spring onions, ginger, chilli,
   garlic and sesame oil, if using, and serve within 1 hour.

smoky tomato salsa

method

THE DELICIOUS **SMOKY FLAVOUR** IN THIS RECIPE COMES FROM BOTH THE SMOKED BACON AND, IF YOU ARE USING IT, THE LIQUID SMOKE **MARINADE**. SERVED WITH SOUR CREAM, THIS SALSA MAKES A GREAT **FILLER** FOR BAKED POTATOES.

1 Skewer the tomatoes on a metal fork and hold them in a gas flame for 1–2 minutes, turning until their skins split and wrinkle. Slip off the skins, halve, discard the seeds, then finely dice the tomato flesh.

2 Cut the bacon into small strips. Heat the oil in a frying pan and cook the bacon for 5 minutes, stirring occasionally, until crisp and browned. Remove from the heat and allow to cool for a few minutes.

3 Mix together the tomatoes, bacon, coriander or parsley, garlic and lime juice. Add the liquid smoke, if using, and salt and pepper to taste.

4 Transfer the salsa to a serving bowl and place in the refrigerator to chill until ready to serve.

ingredients

450g/1lb **tomatoes**
4 rashers **smoked streaky** (fatty) **bacon**
15ml/1 tbsp **vegetable oil**
45ml/3 tbsp chopped fresh **coriander** (cilantro) or **parsley**
1 **garlic** clove, finely chopped
juice of 1 **lime**
15ml/1 tbsp **liquid smoke marinade** (optional)
salt and ground **black pepper**

variations
Give this smoky salsa an extra kick by adding a dash of Tabasco or a pinch of dried chilli flakes.

ingredients

30ml/2 tbsp **peanut oil**

75g/3oz/¾ cup **unsalted peanuts**, blanched

2 **shallots**, chopped

2 **garlic** cloves, chopped

15ml/1 tbsp chopped **fresh root ginger**

1–2 **green chillies,** seeded and thinly sliced

5ml/1 tsp **ground coriander**

1 **lemon grass stalk**, tender base only, chopped

5–10ml/1–2 tsp **light muscovado** (molasses) **sugar**

15ml/1 tbsp **dark soy sauce**

120ml/4fl oz/½ cup canned **coconut milk**

15–30ml/1–2 tbsp **Thai fish sauce** (*nam pla*)

15–30ml/1–2 tbsp **tamarind purée**

lime juice

salt and ground **black pepper**

peanut sauce

THIS IS BASED ON THE FAMOUS **INDONESIAN** SAUCE THAT ACCOMPANIES PORK, CHICKEN OR SHELLFISH **SATAY**. SLIGHTLY THINNED DOWN WITH WATER, IT IS ALSO USED TO DRESS **GADO-GADO**, A WONDERFUL SALAD OF MIXED RAW OR COOKED **VEGETABLES** AND **FRUIT**.

method

SERVES 4–6

1 Heat the oil in a small, heavy-based frying pan and gently fry the peanuts, stirring frequently, until lightly browned. Use a draining spoon to remove the nuts from the pan and drain thoroughly on kitchen paper. Set aside to cool.

2 Add the shallots, garlic, ginger, most of the sliced chillies and the ground coriander to the pan and cook over a low heat, stirring occasionally, for 4–5 minutes, until the shallots are softened but not at all browned.

3 Transfer the spice mixture to a blender or food processor and add the peanuts, lemon grass, 5ml/1 tsp of the sugar, the soy sauce and 105ml/3fl oz/scant ½ cup of the coconut milk and the Thai fish sauce. Blend to form a fairly smooth sauce.

4 Taste and add more fish sauce, together with the tamarind purée, seasoning, lime juice and/or more sugar to taste.

5 Stir in the extra coconut milk and a little water if the sauce seems very thick, but do not let it become runny.

6 Serve the sauce cool or reheat very gently, stirring constantly to prevent it from spitting. Garnish with the remaining sliced green chilli before serving.

spicy corn relish

method

SERVE THIS **SIMPLE** SPICY RELISH WITH
RED ONION RAITA, SWEET MANGO RELISH
AND A **PLATEFUL** OF CRISP ONION BHAJIS
FOR A FABULOUS **INDIAN-STYLE** STARTER.

1 Chop the onion, chilli and garlic. Heat the vegetable oil in a large frying pan and cook the onion, chilli and garlic over a high heat for 5 minutes, until the onions are just beginning to brown.

2 Stir in the mustard seeds and curry powder, then cook for a further 2 minutes, stirring, until the mustard seeds start to splutter and the onions are browned.

3 Remove the fried onion mixture from the heat and allow to cool. Place in a glass bowl. Drain the sweetcorn and stir into the onion mixture.

4 Add the lime rind and juice, coriander and salt and pepper to taste. Cover and serve at room temperature.

ingredients

1 large **onion**
1 **red chilli**, seeded
2 **garlic** cloves
30ml/2 tbsp **vegetable oil**
5ml/1 tsp **black mustard
    seeds**
10ml/2 tsp **hot curry powder**
320g/11¼oz can **sweetcorn**
grated rind and juice of 1 **lime**
45ml/3 tbsp chopped fresh
    coriander (cilantro)
salt and ground **black pepper**

ingredients

3 large **onions**

50g/2oz/4 tbsp **butter**

30ml/2 tbsp **olive oil**

30ml/2 tbsp light **muscovado**
　　(molasses) **sugar**

30ml/2 tbsp **pickled capers**

30ml/2 tbsp chopped
　　fresh **parsley**

salt and ground **black pepper**

cook's tip
Try making this recipe with red
onions or shallots for a subtle
variation in flavour.

toffee onion relish

SLOW AND **GENTLE COOKING** REDUCES
THE ONIONS TO A SOFT, CARAMELIZED
RELISH. **SERVE** WITH ROUND GOAT'S CHEESE
AS A **FIRST COURSE** OR USE AS A **PIQUANT**
RELISH FOR STEAKS.

method

SERVES 4

1 Peel the onions and halve them vertically, through the core, then
slice them thinly. Heat the butter and oil together in a large pan.
Add the onions and sugar and cook very gently for 30 minutes over
a low heat, stirring occasionally, until reduced to a soft rich brown
toffeed mixture.

2 Roughly chop the capers and stir into the toffee onions. Allow the
mixture to cool completely.

3 Stir in the chopped parsley and add salt and pepper to taste. Cover
and chill until ready to serve.

barbecued corn salsa

THE **SMOKY** FLAVOUR OF THE CORN GOES PERFECTLY WITH A **JUICY** PORK OR GAMMON STEAK. SERVE THIS SUCCULENT **SALSA** AT A **BARBECUE** FOR A REAL TREAT.

method

SERVES 4

1 Remove the husks and silky threads covering the corn cobs. Brush the cobs with the melted butter.

2 Gently barbecue or grill (broil) the corn cobs for 20–30 minutes, turning occasionally, until they are tender and tinged brown. To remove the kernels, stand each cob upright on a chopping board and use a large, heavy knife to slice down the length of the cob.

3 Skewer the tomatoes in turn on a metal fork and hold in a gas flame for 1–2 minutes, turning until the skin splits and wrinkles. Slip off the skin and dice the tomato flesh.

4 Finely chop the spring onions and garlic, then mix with the corn and tomato in a small bowl.

5 Stir the lemon juice and olive oil together, adding Tabasco sauce, salt and ground black pepper to taste. Pour the sauce over the salsa and stir well. Cover the salsa and leave to infuse at room temperature for 1–2 hours before serving.

ingredients

2 **corn cobs**
30ml/2 tbsp melted **butter**
4 **tomatoes**
6 **spring onions** (scallions)
1 **garlic** clove
30ml/2 tbsp fresh **lemon juice**
30ml/2 tbsp **olive oil**
red Tabasco sauce, to taste
salt and ground **black pepper**

cook's tip
Make this salsa in summer when fresh cobs of corn are more readily available.

plantain salsa

HERE IS A **SUMMERY** SALSA THAT IS PERFECT FOR **LAZY OUTDOOR EATING**. SERVE WITH TORTILLA OR CORN CHIPS, FOR **DIPPING**.

ingredients

knob of **butter**
4 ripe **plantains**
handful of fresh **coriander**
   (cilantro), plus extra to garnish
30ml/2 tbsp **olive oil**
5ml/1 tsp **cayenne pepper**
salt and ground **black pepper**

cook's tip
Be sure to choose ripe plantains with blackened skins for this recipe as they will be at their sweetest and tenderest.

method

SERVES 4

1 Preheat the oven to 200°C/400°F/Gas 6. Grease four pieces of foil with the knob of butter.

2 Peel the plantains and place one on each piece of foil. Fold the foil over tightly to form a parcel.

3 Bake the plantains for 25 minutes, until tender. Alternatively, the plantains may be cooked in the embers of a charcoal barbecue.

4 Allow the parcels to cool slightly, then remove the plantains, discarding any liquid, and place in a blender or food processor.

5 Process the plantains with the coriander until fairly smooth. Stir in the olive oil, cayenne pepper and salt and pepper to taste.

6 Serve immediately, as the salsa will discolour and over-thicken if left to cool for too long. Garnish with torn coriander leaves.

ingredients

1 **lime**

2 pieces **stem** (preserved) **ginger**

450g/1lb **cherry tomatoes**

115g/4oz/½ cup dark **muscovado** (molasses) **sugar**

100ml/3½fl oz/scant ½ cup **white wine vinegar**

5ml/1 tsp **salt**

variation

If preferred, use ordinary tomatoes, roughly chopped, in place of the cherry tomatoes.

tart tomato relish

THE WHOLE **LIME** USED IN THIS RECIPE ADDS A **PLEASANTLY SOUR** TASTE. SERVE WITH GRILLED OR ROAST **PORK** OR **LAMB**.

method

SERVES 4

1 Use a small sharp knife to slice the whole lime thinly, then chop it into small pieces; do not remove the rind.

2 Coarsely chop the stem ginger. Place the ginger, chopped lime, cherry tomatoes, sugar, white wine vinegar and salt together in a large pan.

3 Bring the tomato relish to the boil, stirring it constantly until the sugar is completely dissolved.

4 Simmer rapidly for about 45 minutes, stirring regularly, until the liquid is evaporated. The relish should have become thickened and pulpy.

5 Allow the mixture to cool for about 5 minutes, then spoon it into sterilized jars. Cool the relish completely, then cover the jars and store in the refrigerator for up to 1 month.

melting cheese dip

method

THIS IS A CLASSIC **FONDUE** IN TRUE SWISS STYLE. IT SHOULD BE SERVED WITH CUBES OF **CRUSTY**, DAY-OLD **BREAD**, BUT IT IS ALSO GOOD WITH CHUNKS OF **SPICY**, CURED **SAUSAGE** SUCH AS CHORIZO.

1 Place the garlic and wine in a small pan and bring gently to the boil. Simmer for 3–4 minutes.

2 Coarsely grate the cheese and stir it into the wine. Continue to stir as the cheese melts.

3 Blend the cornflour to a smooth paste with the Kirsch and pour into the pan, stirring. Bring to the boil, stirring continuously, until the sauce is smooth and thickened.

4 Add salt and pepper to taste. Serve immediately or, better still, transfer to a fondue pan and place over a spirit burner to keep it hot. Garnish with black pepper.

ingredients

1 **garlic** clove, finely chopped

150ml/¼ pint/⅔ cup **dry white wine**

150g/5oz **Gruyère cheese**

5ml/1 tsp **cornflour** (cornstarch)

15ml/1 tbsp **Kirsch**

salt and ground **black pepper**

cook's tip
Gruyère is a tasty cheese that melts incredibly well. Don't be tempted to substitute other cheeses.

red onion, garlic & lemon relish

THIS POWERFUL RELISH IS FLAVOURED WITH **NORTH-AFRICAN** SPICES AND **PUNCHY** PRESERVED LEMONS, AVAILABLE FROM DELICATESSENS AND LARGER SUPERMARKETS OR FROM **MIDDLE-EASTERN** FOOD STORES.

ingredients

45ml/3 tbsp **olive oil**

3 large **red onions**, sliced

2 heads of **garlic**, separated into cloves and peeled

10ml/2 tsp **coriander seeds**, crushed but not finely ground

10ml/2 tsp **light muscovado** (molasses) **sugar**, plus a little extra (optional)

pinch of **saffron threads**

10cm/4in piece **cinnamon stick**

2–3 small whole **dried red chillies** (optional)

2 fresh **bay leaves**

30–45ml/2–3 tbsp **sherry vinegar**

juice of ½ small **orange**

30ml/2 tbsp chopped **preserved lemon**

salt and ground **black pepper**

method

SERVES 6

1 Heat the oil in a heavy pan. Add the onions and stir, then cover and reduce the heat to the lowest setting. Cook for 10–15 minutes, stirring occasionally, until the onions are soft.

2 Add the garlic cloves and coriander seeds. Cover and cook for a further 5–8 minutes until the garlic cloves are soft.

3 Add a pinch of salt, lots of pepper and 10ml/2 tsp sugar, and cook, uncovered, for about 5 minutes. Soak the saffron in about 45ml/ 3 tbsp warm water for 5 minutes, then add to the onions, with the soaking water. Add the cinnamon stick, dried chillies, if using, and bay leaves. Stir in 30ml/2 tbsp of the sherry vinegar and the orange juice.

4 Cook over a low heat, uncovered, until the onions are very soft and most of the liquid has evaporated. Stir in the preserved lemon and cook gently for a further 5 minutes. Taste and adjust the seasoning, adding more salt, sugar and/or vinegar to taste.

5 Serve warm or cold, but not hot or chilled. The relish tastes best if it is allowed to stand for 24 hours.

aromatic & appetizing

basil & lemon mayonnaise

THIS DIP IS MADE FROM **FRESH** MAYONNAISE FLAVOURED WITH LEMON JUICE AND TWO TYPES OF **BASIL**. SERVE WITH SALADS, BAKED POTATOES OR AS A **DELICIOUS** DIP FOR FRENCH FRIES.

method

SERVES 4

1 Place the egg yolks and lemon juice in a blender or food processor and process them briefly until lightly blended.

2 In a jug, stir together both oils. With the machine running, pour in the oil very slowly, a little at a time.

3 Once half of the oil has been added, the remaining oil can be incorporated more quickly. Continue processing to form a thick, creamy mayonnaise.

4 Peel and crush the garlic cloves. Alternatively, place them on a chopping board and sprinkle with salt, then flatten them with the heel of a heavy-bladed knife and chop the flesh. Flatten the garlic again to make a coarse purée.

5 Tear both types of basil into small pieces and stir most of the leaves into the mayonnaise with the crushed garlic.

6 Season with salt and pepper, then transfer to a serving dish. Cover and chill until ready to serve, garnished with the remaining basil.

ingredients

2 large (US extra large) **egg yolks**
15ml/1 tbsp **lemon juice**
150ml/¼ pint/⅔ cup **olive oil**
150ml/¼ pint/⅔ cup **sunflower oil**
4 **garlic** cloves
handful of **green basil leaves**
handful of **opal basil leaves**
salt and grated **black pepper**

cook's tip
Before you start, make sure all the ingredients are at room temperature to help prevent the mayonnaise from curdling.

pesto salsa

method

THIS **AROMATIC** SALSA IS DELICIOUS EITHER DRIZZLED OVER FISH AND CHICKEN, TOSSED WITH **PASTA RIBBONS** OR USED TO DRESS A FRESH AVOCADO AND TOMATO SALAD. TO **TRANSFORM** IT INTO A **DIP**, **MIX** THE PESTO SALSA WITH A LITTLE MAYONNAISE OR SOUR CREAM.

1 Process the fresh coriander and parsley in a blender or food processor until finely chopped.

2 Halve the chillies lengthways and remove their seeds. Add to the herbs together with the garlic and process until finely chopped.

3 Add the pistachio nuts to the herb mixture and pulse the power until they are roughly chopped. Stir in the Parmesan cheese, olive oil and lime juice.

4 Add salt and pepper, to taste. Spoon the mixture into a serving bowl and cover and chill until ready to serve.

ingredients

50g/2oz fresh **coriander**
  (cilantro)
15g/½oz fresh **parsley**
2 **red chillies**
1 **garlic** clove
50g/2oz/⅓ cup shelled
  pistachio nuts
25g/1oz/⅓ cup finely grated
  Parmesan cheese
90ml/6 tbsp **olive oil**
juice of 2 **limes**
salt and ground **black pepper**

variations

Any number of different herbs or nuts may be used to make a similar salsa to this one – try a mixture of rosemary and parsley, or add a handful of black olives.

yellow tomato & orange pepper salsa

SERVE THIS **SUNNY SALSA** AS A DELICIOUS ACCOMPANIMENT TO **SPICY SAUSAGES**, OR GRILLED OR BARBECUED **MEATS**.

ingredients

4 **yellow tomatoes**

1 **orange** (bell) **pepper**

4 **spring onions** (scallions),
   plus extra to garnish

handful of fresh **coriander**
   (cilantro) **leaves**

juice of 1 **lime**

salt and ground **black pepper**

variation

Try using a selection of tomatoes, such as plum or cherry, for a variety of textures and flavours.

method

SERVES 4

1 Halve the tomatoes. Scoop out the seeds with a teaspoon and discard. Finely chop the flesh.

2 Spear the orange pepper on a metal fork and turn it in a gas flame for 1–2 minutes until the skin blisters and chars.

3 Peel off and discard the skin. Remove the core and scrape out the seeds. Finely chop the flesh.

4 Finely chop the spring onions and coriander, then mix both with the pepper and tomato flesh.

5 Squeeze over the lime juice and add salt and pepper to taste. Toss well to mix.

6 Transfer the salsa to a bowl and chill until ready to serve. Garnish with shreds of spring onion.

italian herb salsa

method

THIS SIMPLE **SAUCE** IS A PURÉE OF **FRESH HERBS** BLENDED WITH OLIVE OIL AND PIQUANT FLAVOURINGS. IT IS VERY GOOD WITH ROAST **BEEF AND CHICKEN**, AND TASTES WONDERFUL WITH **POLENTA**.

1 Process the garlic, parsley, basil, mint or coriander, chives, capers, anchovies, mustard and 15ml/1 tbsp of the olive oil in a blender or food processor.

2 Gradually add the remaining oil in a thin stream with the blender or processor motor running.

3 Transfer to a bowl and adjust the seasoning to taste – there should be enough salt from the capers and anchovies. Add a little lemon juice and rind if you like (especially if serving with fish). Serve immediately.

ingredients

1–2 **garlic** cloves, finely chopped

25g/1oz **flat leaf parsley** leaves

15g/½oz fresh **basil**, **mint** or **coriander** (cilantro) or a mixture of herbs

15ml/1 tbsp chopped **chives**

15ml/1 tbsp **salted capers**, rinsed

5 **anchovy fillets** in olive oil, drained and rinsed

10ml/2 tsp **French mustard**

120ml/4fl oz/½ cup **extra virgin olive oil**

a little grated **lemon** rind and juice (optional)

ground **black pepper**

variations ..

Whisk in 30–45ml/2–3 tbsp crème fraîche to make a mild sauce that goes well with polenta, cauliflower and potatoes.

Substitute fresh chervil, tarragon, dill or fennel for the herbs used here to make a sauce that goes particularly well with lightly poached or baked fish, such as hake or sea bass.

roasted tomato salsa

ROASTING THE TOMATOES GIVES A GREATER DEPTH TO THE **FLAVOUR** OF THIS VERSATILE SALSA, WHICH ALSO BENEFITS FROM THE **WARM**, **ROUNDED** FLAVOUR OF ROASTED CHILLIES. SERVE WITH FISH OR MEAT.

method

SERVES 6

1 Preheat the oven to 200°C/400°F/Gas 6. Cut the tomatoes into quarters and place them in a roasting tin. Add the chillies.

2 Roast for 45 minutes–1 hour, until the tomatoes and chillies are charred and have softened.

3 Place the roasted chillies in a strong plastic bag. Tie the top to keep the steam in and set aside for 20 minutes. Leave the tomatoes to cool slightly, then remove the skins and dice the flesh.

4 Chop the onion finely, then place in a bowl and add the lime juice and the chopped tomatoes.

5 Remove the chillies from the bag and peel off the skins. Cut off the stalks, then slit the chillies and scrape out the seeds with a sharp knife. Chop the chillies roughly and add them to the onion mixture. Mix well.

6 Chop the coriander and add most to the salsa. Add salt, cover and chill for at least 1 hour before serving, sprinkled with the remaining coriander. This salsa will keep in the refrigerator for 1 week.

ingredients

500g/1¼lb **tomatoes**

2 green **chillies**

1 **onion**

juice of 1 **lime**

large bunch of fresh **coriander**
(cilantro)

salt

cook's tip

Use plum tomatoes or vine tomatoes, which have more flavour than those that have been grown for their keeping properties rather than their flavour. Cherry tomatoes are also good in this salsa, and there is no need to peel them after roasting.

fresh tomato & tarragon salsa

PLUM TOMATOES, GARLIC, OLIVE OIL AND **BALSAMIC VINEGAR** MAKE FOR A VERY **MEDITERRANEAN SALSA** – TRY SERVING THIS WITH **LAMB CUTLETS** OR TOSS IT WITH FRESHLY COOKED **PASTA**.

ingredients

8 **plum tomatoes**
1 small **garlic** clove
60ml/4 tbsp **olive oil**
15ml/1 tbsp **balsamic vinegar**
30ml/2 tbsp finely chopped fresh
   tarragon, plus extra
   to garnish
salt and ground **black pepper**

cook's tip
Be sure to serve this salsa at room temperature as the tomatoes taste less sweet, and rather acidic, when they are chilled.

method

SERVES 4

1 Skewer the tomatoes in turn on a metal fork and hold in a gas flame for 1–2 minutes, turning until the skin splits and wrinkles.

2 Slip off the tomato skins and finely chop the flesh. Using a sharp knife, crush or finely chop the garlic.

3 Whisk together the olive oil, balsamic vinegar and plenty of salt and pepper.

4 Stir the main batch of finely chopped tarragon into the olive oil and balsamic vinegar mixture.

5 Mix the tomatoes and garlic in a bowl and pour the tarragon dressing over. Leave to infuse for at least 1 hour before serving at room temperature. Garnish with shredded tarragon leaves.

orange & chive salsa

FRESH CHIVES AND **SWEET** ORANGES UNITE TO PROVIDE A VERY **CHEERFUL** COMBINATION OF COLOURS AND FLAVOURS.

method

SERVES 4

1 Begin by slicing the bottom off the orange so that it will stand firmly on a chopping board.

2 Using a large sharp knife, remove the orange peel by slicing from the top to the bottom of the fruit.

3 Hold the orange in one hand over a bowl. Slice towards the middle of the fruit, to one side of a segment, and then gently twist the knife to ease the segment away from the membrane and out of the orange. Repeat to remove all the segments. Squeeze any juice from the remaining membrane. Prepare the second orange in the same way.

4 Roughly chop the orange segments and place them in the bowl with the collected juice.

5 Halve the tomato and use a teaspoon to scoop the seeds into the bowl. Finely dice the flesh and add to the oranges in the bowl.

6 Hold the bunch of chives neatly together and use a pair of kitchen scissors to snip them into the bowl.

7 Thinly slice the garlic clove and stir it into the orange mixture. Pour over the olive oil, season with sea salt and stir well to mix. Serve the salsa within 2 hours.

ingredients

2 large **oranges**
1 **beefsteak tomato**
bunch of **chives**
1 **garlic** clove
30ml/2 tbsp **olive oil**
sea salt

cook's tip
Add a little diced mozzarella cheese to make a more substantial salsa.

low-fat saffron dip

method

SERVE THIS MILD-FLAVOURED DIP WITH **FRESH**, CRISP **VEGETABLE CRUDITES** – IT IS PARTICULARLY GOOD WITH SOME LITTLE FLORETS OF **CAULIFLOWER**, TINY WHOLE CARROTS, ASPARAGUS AND BABY **CORN**.

1 Pour the boiling water into a small container and add the saffron threads. Leave to infuse for 3 minutes.

2 Beat the fromage frais or ricotta cheese until it is smooth, then stir in the infused saffron liquid.

3 Use a pair of scissors to snip the chives into the dip. Tear the basil leaves into small pieces and stir them in as well.

4 Add salt and ground black pepper to taste. Serve the dip immediately, with the crudités of your choice.

ingredients

15ml/1 tbsp boiling **water**

small pinch of **saffron threads**

200g/7oz/scant 1 cup low-fat **fromage frais** or low-fat **ricotta cheese**

10 fresh **chives**

10 fresh **basil** leaves

salt and ground **black pepper**

variation
For a fresher flavour, leave out the saffron and add a squeeze of lemon or lime juice instead.

fresh & fruity

ingredients

2 large, tart **cooking apples**

30ml/2 tbsp **brandy**

25g/1oz/2 tbsp **butter**

25g/1oz/2 tbsp light **muscovado**
(molasses) **sugar**

variation
Stir in a handful of small, plump
sultanas (golden raisins) with the
diced apple.

sweet apple sauce

THIS **BUTTERY** APPLE SAUCE CAN BE SERVED
WARM OR COLD WITH ROAST **PORK OR LAMB**.

method   SERVES 4

1 Using a sharp knife, peel, core and finely dice the cooking apples.
Place in a small pan with the brandy, butter and sugar.

2 Heat gently, stirring, until the sugar dissolves. Cover and allow to
simmer very gently for 20–25 minutes, until the apple mixture has
become thick and pulpy.

3 Allow the sauce to cool completely. Cover and store in the refrigerator
for up to 5 days.

cook's tip
Look for firm and unblemished apples. Store them in a cool, dry place
and use within 2 weeks.

sweet potato salsa

THIS **COLOURFUL** AND DELIGHTFULLY **SWEET** SALSA MAKES THE PERFECT ACCOMPANIMENT TO **HOT**, **SPICY** MEXICAN DISHES. ALTERNATIVELY, SERVE WITH CORN CHIPS AND WEDGES OF VEGETABLES, FOR DIPPING.

method

SERVES 4

1 Use a sharp knife to peel the sweet potatoes and dice the flesh finely. Bring a pan of water to the boil. Add the sweet potato and cook for 8–10 minutes, until just soft.

2 Drain off the water, cover the pan and put it back on the hob, having first turned off the heat. Leave the sweet potato for about 5 minutes to dry out, then tip into a bowl and set aside.

3 Mix the orange juice and crushed dried chillies in a bowl. Chop the spring onions finely and add them to the juice and chillies.

4 When the sweet potatoes are cool, add the orange juice mixture and toss carefully until all the pieces are coated.

5 Cover the bowl and chill the sweet potato salsa for at least 1 hour in the refrigerator.

6 Taste, and season with salt and ground black pepper if necessary. Stir in the lime juice if you prefer a fresher taste. The salsa will keep for 2–3 days in a covered bowl in the refrigerator.

ingredients

675g/1½lb **sweet potatoes**
juice of 1 small **orange**
5ml/1 tsp crushed dried
jalapeño chillies
4 small **spring onions** (scallions)
juice of 1 small **lime** (optional)
salt and ground **black pepper**

---

cook's tip
This fresh and tasty salsa is also very good served with a simple grilled (broiled) salmon fillet or other fish dishes, and makes a delicious accompaniment to veal escalopes or grilled chicken breasts.

mango & red onion salsa

A VERY **SIMPLE FRUITY SALSA**, WHICH IS **LIVENED UP** BY THE ADDITION OF SWEET **PASSION FRUIT** PULP.

ingredients

1 large ripe **mango**

1 **red onion**

2 **passion fruit**

6 large fresh **basil** leaves

juice of 1 **lime**, to taste

sea salt

---

variation

Sweetcorn kernels are a delicious addition to this salsa.

---

method

SERVES 4

1 Holding the mango upright on a chopping board, use a large knife to slice the flesh away carefully from either side of the large flat stone in two portions.

2 Using a smaller knife, trim away any flesh still clinging to the top and bottom of the stone.

3 Score the flesh of the mango halves deeply, taking care to avoid cutting through the skin: make parallel incisions about 1cm/½ in apart; turn and cut lines in the opposite direction. Carefully turn the skin inside out so the flesh stands out like hedgehog spikes. Slice the dice away from the skin.

4 Finely chop the red onion and place it in a serving bowl with the diced mango.

5 Halve the passion fruit, scoop out the seeds and pulp, and add to the mango mixture.

6 Tear the basil leaves coarsely and stir them into the salsa with lime juice and a little sea salt to taste. Serve immediately.

aromatic peach & cucumber salsa

ANGOSTURA BITTERS ADD A MOST UNUSUAL AND VERY PLEASING FLAVOUR TO THIS SALSA. THE **DISTINCTIVE**, SWEET-TASTING MINT COMPLEMENTS **CHICKEN** AND OTHER MAIN **MEAT DISHES**.

ingredients

2 **peaches**
1 mini **cucumber**
2.5ml/½ tsp **Angostura bitters**
15ml/1 tbsp **olive oil**
10ml/2 tsp fresh **lemon juice**
30ml/2 tbsp chopped fresh **mint**
salt and ground **black pepper**

cook's tip
The texture of the peach and the crispness of the cucumber will fade fairly rapidly, so try to prepare this salsa as close to the serving time as possible.

method

SERVES 4

1 Using a small sharp knife, carefully score a line right around the circumference of each peach, cutting just through the skin.

2 Bring a large pan of water to the boil. Add the peaches and blanch them for 60 seconds. Drain and briefly refresh in cold water.

3 Peel off and discard the skin. Halve the peaches and remove their stones. Finely dice the flesh and place in a bowl.

4 Trim the ends off the cucumber, then finely dice the flesh and stir it into the peaches.

5 Stir the Angostura bitters, olive oil and lemon juice together and then stir this dressing into the peach mixture.

6 Stir in the chopped mint with salt and pepper to taste. Chill and serve within 1 hour.

variations
Nectarines can be used instead of peaches, or try diced mango instead for an alternative flavour.

ingredients

1 small orange-fleshed **melon,**
such as Charentais melon

1 large wedge **watermelon**

2 **oranges**

prosciutto, to serve

---

variation

Other melons can also be used for
this salsa. For example, try
cantaloupe or Ogen melon.

mixed melon salsa

A **COMBINATION** OF TWO VERY DIFFERENT
MELONS GIVES THIS SALSA AN **EXCITING**
FLAVOUR AND **TEXTURE**. IT'S GREAT SERVED
WITH COLD MEATS SUCH AS PROSCIUTTO.

method

SERVES 8

1 Quarter the orange-fleshed melon and pick out the seeds. Use a large,
sharp knife to cut off the skin and dice the flesh. Remove the seeds
and the skin from the watermelon. Dice the flesh into small chunks.

2 Use a citrus fruit zester to pare long strips of rind from both of
the oranges. Cut both of the oranges in half and then squeeze out all
their juice into a bowl.

3 Mix both types of melon with the orange rind and juice. Chill for about
30 minutes and serve.

ingredients

- 2 large **mangoes**
- 1 **cooking apple**
- 2 **shallots**
- 4cm/1½in piece **fresh root ginger**
- 2 **garlic** cloves
- 115g/4oz/1 cup small **sultanas** (golden raisins)
- 2 **star anise**
- 5ml/1 tsp ground **cinnamon**
- 2.5ml/½ tsp dried **chilli flakes**
- 2.5ml/½ tsp **salt**
- 175ml/6fl oz/¾ cup **cider vinegar**
- 130g/4½oz/scant ½ cup light **muscovado** (molasses) **sugar**

variations
Select alternative spices to suit your own taste: for example, add juniper berries in place of the star anise or try cumin seeds.

sweet mango relish

STIR A **SPOONFUL** OF THIS RELISH INTO **SOUPS AND STEWS** FOR ADDED FLAVOUR OR SERVE IT WITH A WEDGE OF **CHEDDAR CHEESE** AND CHUNKS OF CRUSTY BREAD.

method

MAKES 750ML/1¼ PINTS/3 CUPS

1 Hold the mangoes, one at a time, upright on a chopping board and use a large knife to slice the flesh away from either side of the large flat stone in two portions.

2 Using a smaller knife, carefully trim away any flesh still clinging to the top and bottom of the mango stone.

3 Score the flesh of the mango halves deeply, taking care to avoid cutting through the skin: make parallel incisions about 1cm/½in apart; turn and cut lines in the opposite direction. Carefully turn the skin inside out so the flesh stands out like hedgehog spikes. Slice the dice away from the skin.

4 Using a sharp knife, peel and roughly chop the apple, shallots, fresh root ginger and garlic.

5 Place the mango, apple, shallots, ginger, garlic and sultanas in a large pan. Add the spices, salt, vinegar and sugar.

6 Bring to the boil, stirring until the sugar dissolves. Reduce the heat and simmer gently for 45 minutes, stirring occasionally, until the relish has reduced and thickened.

7 Allow the relish to cool for 5 minutes, then pot it into clean jars. Cool completely, cover and store in the refrigerator for up to 2 months.

papaya & coconut dip

SWEET AND **SMOOTH PAPAYA** TEAMS UP WELL WITH GINGER AND CREME FRAICHE TO MAKE A **LUSCIOUS** SWEET DIP.

ingredients

method

SERVES 6

2 ripe **papayas**

200ml/7fl oz/scant 1 cup **crème fraîche**

1 piece **stem** (preserved) **ginger**

fresh **coconut**, to decorate

cook's tip

If fresh coconut is not available, you could substitute coconut strands. Toast lightly in a hot oven until golden.

1 Halve each papaya lengthways, then scoop out and discard the seeds. Cut a few slices and reserve for decoration.

2 Scoop out the papaya flesh and process it until smooth in a blender or a food processor.

3 Stir in the crème fraîche and process until well blended. Finely chop the stem ginger and stir it into the mixture, then chill until you are ready to serve.

4 Pierce a hole in the "eye" of the coconut and drain off the liquid, then break open the coconut. Hold it securely in one hand and hit it sharply with a hammer.

5 Remove the shell from a piece of coconut, then snap the nut into pieces no wider than 2cm/¾in.

6 Use a swivel-bladed vegetable peeler to shave off 2cm/¾in lengths of coconut. Scatter these over the dip with the reserved papaya before serving.

ingredients

50g/2oz **plain** (semisweet)
  chocolate
2 large ripe **bananas**
15ml/1 tbsp **malt extract**

cook's tip
This smooth dip can be prepared in advance and chilled. When you are ready to serve, stir in some lightly whipped double (heavy) cream to soften and enrich the mixture.

malted chocolate & banana dip

THIS **DELECTABLE** DIP IS **LOVELY** SERVED WITH CHUNKS OF **FRESH FRUIT**. TRY WEDGES OF KIWI FRUIT, THICKLY SLICED **PEACH** AND HALVED **STRAWBERRIES**.

method

SERVES 4

1 Break the plain chocolate into small pieces and place them in a small heatproof bowl. Stand the bowl over a pan of gently simmering water and stir the chocolate occasionally until it melts. Allow to cool.

2 Cut the bananas into pieces and process them in a blender or food processor until finely chopped.

3 With the motor running, pour in the malt extract, and continue processing until the mixture is thick and frothy.

4 Drizzle in the chocolate in a steady stream and process until well blended. Serve immediately.

pineapple & passion fruit salsa

PILE THIS **FRUITY** SALSA INTO **BRANDY SNAP** BASKETS OR **MERINGUE** NESTS.

method

SERVES 6

1 Cut off the top and bottom of the pineapple so that it will stand firmly on a chopping board. Using a large sharp knife, slice off the peel.

2 Carefully cut out the eyes from the pineapple using a small sharp knife. Turn the pineapple on its side and cut into slices. Use a small metal pastry cutter to stamp out the tough core. Finely chop the flesh of the pineapple.

3 Halve both of the passion fruit and use a teaspoon to scoop out the seeds and pulp into a bowl.

4 Stir the chopped pineapple and yogurt into the passion fruit in the bowl. Cover and chill the salsa for at least 30 minutes in the refrigerator.

5 Gently stir in the muscovado sugar just before you are ready to serve the salsa.

ingredients

1 small fresh **pineapple**
2 **passion fruit**
150ml/¼ pint/⅔ cup **Greek**
　(US strained plain) **yogurt**
30ml/2 tbsp light **muscovado**
　(molasses) **sugar**

variation
Lightly whipped double (heavy) cream can be used instead of the yogurt if you prefer.

index